MW01143834

Feeding the Lambs

Lessons of Faith for Children

Feeding the Lambs

Lessons of Faith for Children

by

Mark L. Mongeau

ISBN: 1-58721-763-5

1stBooks – rev. 6/20/00

About the Book

There is no more important duty of parents than to guide their children on the path of faith. All the PTA meetings, soccer games, dance recitals, junior proms and high school graduations in existence are not as important to the development of our children as helping them gain the knowledge of a joyful life with God at its center. The primary responsibility to nurture children in their faith lies with the parents, (mom and dad), and their immediate family. But in the "family of faith," the church, also has a role to provide our children, the lambs among us, with a faith environment within which they can grow and thrive. Through creative Sunday schools, children's choirs, vacation bible schools, etc., we work to instill the knowledge of God and the life that He asks us to live.

This book has been written to provide adult leaders of children's services, (as well as parents), with some ideas to help with learning experiences for their children. They were originally prepared as "Children's Moments," but the ideas in each lesson can easily be used for other opportunities such as devotions, opening thoughts for assemblies or other teaching forms. The format is very simple. A physical object, usually a very common item familiar to the children, is used to connect the leader with the children and to introduce the lesson. Like a parable, the lesson has only one central point. Each lesson takes a basic part of faith life and explains it in a way that a child can understand.

The text of each lesson presented in this book is a guide and shouldn't be repeated word for word. I have borrowed liberally from my own life experience, and the main function of my life examples is to jog the memory of the presenter who can put their own experience, personality, humor and style into the effort; the only bounds are the limits of your creativity.

"Simon son of John, do you love me more than these?" He said to him, "Yes Lord; you know that I love you." Jesus Said to him, *"Feed my lambs."*

There is no more important duty of parents than to guide their children on the path of faith. All the PTA meetings, soccer games, dance recitals, junior proms and high school graduations in existence are not as important to the development of our children as helping them gain the knowledge of a joyful life with God at its center. The primary responsibility to nurture children in their faith lies with the parents, (mom and dad), and their immediate family. But in the "family of faith," the church, also has a role to provide our children, the lambs among us, with a faith environment within which they can grow and thrive. Through creative Sunday schools, children's choirs, vacation bible schools, etc., we work to instill the knowledge of God and the life that He asks us to live.

Many churches include, as part of their program, a special worship service for their younger children. The format and content of these services are as diverse as the churches within which they are held. There is certainly more than one way to reach a child, and many different approaches are needed. In some churches, mine included, the children begin in the regular adult worship service. At a specific point in the service, the children are invited to the front of the sanctuary, where they are led in a "Children's Moment," a brief lesson on a specific topic of faith. Following this lesson they are led to the remainder of their worship service, apart from the sanctuary.

This book has been written to provide adult leaders of children's services, (as well as parents), with some ideas. They were originally prepared as "Children's Moments," but the ideas in each lesson can easily be used for other opportunities such as devotions, opening thoughts for assemblies or other teaching forms. The format is very simple. A physical object, usually a very common item familiar to the children, is used to connect the leader with the children and to introduce the lesson. Like a parable, the lesson has only one central point. Each lesson takes a basic part of faith life and explains it in a way that a child can understand.

I have also included an appropriate Bible verse (New International Version) for each lesson. Depending on the setting, you may have the opportunity to present and talk about the verse, or, if time and the setting don't permit, you may just leave it out.

Each lesson is closed with a prayer. Now, I'm not a big fan of pre-written or pre-prepared prayers. I believe that when we quiet our hearts and go to God in prayer, the right words will flow from our hearts without a great deal of conscious thought. This is, I think, the best sort of prayer conversation. That being said, I have included in each lesson a short "prayer thought." I don't mean for this to be repeated as a closing prayer. But maybe, as you ponder the thought, your mind and heart will "align" to prayer, and you and the children can converse with the Father.

The text of each lesson presented in this book is a guide and shouldn't be repeated word for word. I have borrowed liberally from my own life experience, and the main function of my life examples is to jog the memory of the presenter who can put their own experience, personality, humor and style into the effort; the only bounds are the limits of your creativity. And remember the following important "rules":

- Have fun with it; children like to have fun.
- Children respond better to an adult that is sharing with them, not talking at them.

- Children don't listen the same way that adults do, so don't worry about those who wiggle, squirm or turn around and wave to mom. They are listening, we just don't always notice.
- Don't worry about speaking "over their heads." I've found that children are capable of understanding a lot more then we give them credit for.
- You may not get the reaction you want from all the children and you may feel that you are reaching only one child; congratulations. . . you may just have made a difference in the life of one of God's precious creations.

There are 52 lessons in this book, one for every week of the year. Certainly, feel free to jump around and use them in any order that works. I hope that you use as many as you can, and I pray that you make a difference in the lives of the "lambs" whom God has entrusted to your care.

1

ADVERTISEMENTS

Subject: Trust in God, He never fails

Object Item: An exciting advertisement from the newspaper

Bible Verse: Trust in the Lord and do good; dwell in the land
and enjoy safe pasture. (Psalms 37:3)

Discussion:

The Sunday edition of the newspaper is several times larger
than any of the daily editions. One of the reasons for this is the
many advertising flyers that stores include in the Sunday edition.
I guess they figure that many people spend a good part of their
leisure time on Sunday perusing the paper, and that this is a good
time to try to grab the readers' attention. Boy, oh, boy! Do they
try to grab your attention! They try to outdo one another by
using lots of colors, attractive models and great photographs of
their products.

However, when you go to the store to buy the products, they
never seem to look as good as they do in the flyer. I certainly
don't look as good in the suit that is on sale as the guy that was

wearing it in the ad. There is no question that the people who produce the ads work very hard, and usually succeed, to convince us that their products are better than they really are. It's just like those restaurants that show pictures of their food on the menu. I've never eaten a stack of pancakes or a fried egg that looks nearly as appetizing as it did on the menu.

I guess that the "ad people" are just doing their jobs, but it's frustrating to be disappointed all the time. Fortunately for us, God doesn't work this way. Through His word, the Bible, He tells us about Himself. He tells us that He loves us, and that He will always be there when we need Him. When we go to Him, He is true to His promises. We will never find a substitute that is less than we expect. God can be trusted all the time, in all matters, by all who need His loving care. Amen!

Prayer Thought:

Father, thank you for never letting us down, and help us to always give up ourselves and to trust in you.

2

THE CHAIR

Subject: Stewardship

Object Item: A common chair

Bible Verse: Because of the service by which you have proved yourselves, men will praise God for the obedience that accompanies your confessions of the gospel of Christ and for your generosity in sharing with them and with everyone else. (2 Corinthians 2:13)

Discussion:

Take a close look at a chair. A chair has three main parts. The seat is the part that you sit in. The back is attached to the seat and supports the back of the person seated in the chair. But probably the most important part of a chair is the part that you can see the least; the legs. The legs form the foundation of the chair, supporting the seat. Most chairs have four legs. If even one leg were to break, the person in the chair would fall to the floor.

All of us who belong to a church are, in many ways, like the legs of a chair. We support the church like the legs support the chair. The United Methodist church describes the responsibility of its members to support their church in four ways.

- Prayers: Praying for the church and asking God's blessing on its work
- Presence: Attending church services and participating in opportunities such as Bible studies, Sunday School, etc.
- Gifts: Giving of one's financial resources to pay for the work of he church.
- Service: Working in the name of the church to help those in need and to help the church grow.

Like the legs support the chair, all four of these elements are critical to the support of the church.. If even one is neglected, the church cannot become all that God desires. So, every one of us then must do our part to help support our church. By praying, attending and giving of our money and time, we will be the "legs" that will help our church be what God wants it to be. Amen!

Prayer Thought:

Lord, use me and the gifts that you have given me to help your church do your will.

3

WHO ARE WE ?

Subject: Christian love

Object Item: A diploma and a driver's license

Bible Verse: Be imitators of God, therefore, as dearly loved
children and live a life of love just as Christ loved and gave
Himself up for us as a fragrant offering and sacrifice to God.
(Ephesians 5:1-2)

Discussion:

When a person graduates from high school or college, he/she
receives a diploma. This is a certificate that proves that the
person attended the school and successfully completed the
required course work. I never go anywhere in my car without
my driver's license. The license has my name and picture on it,
and proves to anyone who looks at it that I am licensed to drive a
car.

We have all sorts of certificates, cards and licenses to prove
our membership and ability in all sorts of areas. But how do we

prove that we are followers of Christ? Sure, some of us received a certificate at our baptism, or we have a church membership certificate buried somewhere in a drawer at home. But these things don't prove our commitment to Jesus. It says in the Bible that as Christians we are known by our love; our love for God, each other, and most importantly, for those who do not love us. Jesus loved all people, even those who betrayed Him and delivered Him to His death. As Christians, we are expected by God to love unconditionally; not because the love is returned, but because that's who we are and that it is the right thing for us to do. Amen!

Prayer Thought:

Lord, let your love for me cause me to love others.

4

$\underline{\textbf{\textit{FOOL'S GOLD}}}$

Subject: Real value

Object Item: A piece or picture of iron pyrite (fool's gold)

Bible Verse: Do not store up for yourselves treasures on earth where moth and rust destroy and where thieves break in and steal, but store up your treasures in Heaven. (Matthew 6:19-20)

Discussion:

I was in a gem store one day, browsing around and admiring the many colors of the thousands of gems and pieces of minerals displayed throughout the store. In the corner I saw a large barrel of shiny gold stones.   Upon closer inspection, the stones appeared to be large nuggets of gold ore. However, the sign on the barrel read "Iron Pyrite. . . $2.00 per pound". Obviously, I was looking at a mineral much less valuable than the gold which it resembled.   Iron pyrite is also called "Fool's Gold", since it looks very much like gold, yet it is so commonly found in the earth that it has very little value. Although it appears to be valuable, it is not.

Many things in life appear to be valuable to us. We hold these material things, money, clothes, cars, houses etc., so valuable that we work very hard to accumulate as much as we can. A lot of people judge a person's worth by how many possessions or how much money that they have. Like the "Fool's Gold," these things seem very valuable to us when we get them. But in time they wear out, break, or get used up, and we are left with very little.

The Bible tells us that these things cannot in themselves bring us happiness. Jesus tells us not to store up things on earth where they can be lost, but to concentrate on heavenly treasures. Rather than loading up our material storehouses, God asks us to concentrate on building up our souls by feeding ourselves with His word and truth. By learning about our Lord and His will for us, and then by acting in His will (living in a way that pleases Him), we accumulate things of real value that cannot be taken away, and that will bring us real happiness. Amen!

Prayer Thought:

Dear God, give me a mind that knows the things of true value.

5

<u>*INSIDE OUTSIDE*</u>

Subject: The external aspects of inner goodness

Object Item: A box of Girl Scout cookies

Bible Verse: I am the vine and you are the branches. If a man remains in Me and I in him he will bear much fruit. (John 15:5)

Discussion:

One of my favorite times of the year is February. The weather is turning warmer, Easter is just around the corner and the Girl Scouts are out selling their cookies. These green clad "saleskids" are everywhere: at the mall, standing in front of the supermarket and at your front door. I'm not complaining, I love these cookies. My favorite type is Thin Mint followed closely by Peanut Butter.

The cookie boxes are also very interesting. They have pictures of Girl Scouts doing their thing. The boxes also reveal the contents, along with the nutritional information about the cookies (why they print this I don't quite understand). You can tell exactly what is inside the box by reading the outside.

The outside of the box tells you about the inside. But how can you tell what is inside a person, what is in their heart? The old hymn tells us that "They will know we are Christians by our love." Jesus said that we will be known by the fruit that we bear. What does this mean? If our hearts are filled with God's love, we will show that love by sharing it with others, and giving of ourselves to help those who God would have us help; the poor, needy and hurting. Our actions, in God's name, on the outside will reflect God's love that we carry inside. Amen!

Prayer Thought:

Lord, may my deeds reflect the faith that I have in my heart.

6

NEW THINGS

Subject: Life with Christ is forever new

Object Item: Something new

Bible Verse: Therefore, if anyone is in Christ, he is a new creation; the old has gone and the new has come. (2 Corinthians 5:17)

Discussion:

Did you ever ride in a new car? I can't think of anything that smells quite as good as the inside of a new car. That unmistakable combination of vinyl and plastic just screams, "I'm brand new, drive me!" When I get to heaven, I'm sure that it is going to smell either like my wife's brownies or a new car.

I love new things. Is there anything quite like a new set of sheets? When I slip into a bed with new sheets I try not to fall asleep lest I miss the experience. A newly laundered, starched shirt gives me confidence that I look my best. And no experience is more enthralling than opening a new jar of peanut butter, inhaling the aroma, and taking the first scoop from the smooth surface.

The problem with new things is that they quickly become old. The new car, in a few years, becomes an irritating clunker, new sheets and shirts become soiled and eventually are good only for Halloween costumes and cleaning rags. And, alas, the peanut butter from the bottom of the jar just doesn't taste as good as the first scoop.

When we first meet Jesus and ask Him into our lives, we are, as the Bible says, new creatures. We enter into a new life with Christ. But unlike material things which eventually wear out and get old, our relationship with Jesus gets more wonderful every day. By studying God's word and speaking to Him often in prayer, we have our hearts opened to an ever growing portion of His love, every day, making our experience ever new! Amen!

Prayer Thought:

Dear God, as I grow in my faith, help me to look at each day as a new opportunity to serve you.

7

<u>QUALIFICATIONS</u>

Subject: God's love is unconditional

Object Item: Employment section of a newspaper

Bible Verse: But I tell you, love your enemies and pray for those who persecute you, that you may be sons of your Father in Heaven. (Matthew 5:44)

Discussion:

Look at the Employment Section, or "Want Ads" of a newspaper. They are filled with hundreds of companies advertising for people to come to work for them. Most of the ads list the qualifications of the people that will fill the position. An ad for a secretary may require certain typing skills, an ad for an accountant may require a college education and a company looking for a delivery driver will most likely require that applicants have a valid drivers license.

Lots of things in life require people to qualify. Certain rides at amusement parks have height requirements for the people who use them. Some restaurants require that male diners wear jackets and ties. Many of the things that we do are qualified. Unfortunately, some people qualify the love that they give to others. Consider the following;

I'll love you only if you love me.

I'll love you if you do something for me or give something to me.

I'll love you only if you agree with me.

I'll love you only if you are just like me and share my lifestyle.

Thankfully, God is not like this. God loves us regardless of anything else. His love is unqualified. There are no "ifs" in God's love. Even if we do not return His love, or we disobey His word, God loves us. And because He loves us like this, we can love others in the same way. Amen!

Prayer Thought:

Lord, thank you for loving me, even when I am not very lovable.

8

SEEDS

Subject: Giving of ourselves

Object Item: Pack of seeds

Bible Verse: Remember this: whoever sows sparingly will reap sparingly and whoever sows generously will also reap generously. (2 Corinthians 9:6)

Discussion:

Take a close look at a pack of seeds. Because the seeds are so small, a small envelope can hold hundreds, even thousands of seeds. What happens when you plant only one small seed? After a while a full grown flower or plant will be created. If you were to plant two seeds you would create two plants; three seeds produce three plants and so on. If you were to plant a whole pack of seeds, hundreds of plants would appear.

When we do a good deed, or give of ourselves, we are planting a seed. In a while, that deed will bear fruit in some way. The person that we help will feel better, and this in itself is good fruit. Also, this person may later, in turn, give of <u>him</u>self and perform a good deed of his own. Not to mention that just the act of giving is good for the soul of the giver. So if doing one deed is like planting one seed, how much better it is to plant many seeds by continually giving of ourselves. As the Bible says, "We will reap that which we sow." If we "sow" by giving of ourselves often, what a wonderful harvest will we all reap! Amen!

Prayer Thought:

Father, help me to be a generous giver of your love.

9

TRIVIA

Subject: The importance of God's word

Object Item: A Trivial Pursuit game and a Bible

Bible Verse: . . . and how from infancy you have known the holy Scriptures, which are able to make you wise for salvations through faith in Christ Jesus. (2 Timothy 3:15)

Discussion:

One of my favorite board games is Trivial Pursuit. My family will sometimes spend hours playing this game. I never fail to learn several pieces of relatively useless information every time I play this game. Actually, the definition of trivia is more or less useless information. I'm actually pretty good at this game, because my mind seems to be pretty amenable to trivial information. Although the game is quite enjoyable, those who play it really don't learn much of any great significance.

In contrast to the Trivial Pursuit game, take a close look at the Bible. Most of the information in the game is useless, while

<u>all</u> of the information in the Bible is extremely important. In fact, there is no trivia in the Bible. This is the receptacle of God's word, and it is here for us to learn and understand more about God and what He wants for us in our lives. We should, therefore, read and study God's word as often as possible. Studying the Bible is a "Not So Trivial Pursuit." Amen!

Prayer Thought:

Lord God, open my heart to the teaching of your word.

10

YARN

Subject: Our lives in God's hands

Object Item: A ball of yarn and a completed knitted item.

Bible Verse: Yet O Lord, you are our Father. We are the clay, you are the potter; we are all the work of your hand. (Isaiah 64:8)

Discussion:

You can do some interesting things with a ball of yarn. You can play with a kitten, tie knots and other fun things like that. I remember a time when one of my children thought that taking one end of a ball of yarn and running around the house would be fun. By the time I caught her, she had created a veritable web of yarn throughout our house. When I was a young child, my mother would have me stand for what seemed like hours, arms outstretched holding a new package of yarn, while she rolled it into a ball for her knitting projects. Yarn can indeed be interesting.

But in the hands of a master craftsman or artist, the yarn can be much more than a plaything. It can be made into a beautiful work. In a similar way, a potter can turn a lump of clay into a finished piece of pottery. Our lives are like the yarn or the unformed clay. If we put our lives in the hands of the Master, God, He will make a beautiful work of our lives. Amen!

Prayer Thought:

Lord, make me one that can do your work and will.

11

BLUBERRIES

Subject: Love's versatility

Object Item: A bag of blueberries

Bible Verse: A new command I give you; love one another. As I have loved you, so you must love one another. (John 13:34)

Discussion:

I love blueberries! I love to pick them and eat them fresh off the bush. When picking blueberries with my family, I am always the last to fill my bucket. Although I can pick faster than any of them, I usually eat one berry for every two that I put in the bucket.

The thing about blueberries that I like the best is their versatility. You can do so much with them. My wife can take a bag of blueberries and make a pie, cobbler, pancakes, muffins and preserves. Sometimes she makes a hot blueberry compote and we pour it hot over vanilla ice cream. They sell blueberry bagels at the local bagel shop and blueberry jam and jelly at the supermarket. Let's not forget just popping them plain or putting them on your *Special K* in the morning. I can't think of another fruit that is quite as versatile as blueberries.

Speaking of versatility, love is very versatile. The ancient Greeks knew this. Unlike the English language, that has only one word to define this emotion, Greek has at least four separate words to describe the various aspects of love. You can love your house, dog, sister, parents, spouse and fellow man in very different ways. Also, love can effect every situation differently. When you express love to a sad friend, they feel better. Express love to a happy friend, and you are able to share and enhance the joy. You express love to someone in need by helping to meet the need. And you can show love to someone helping you by accepting their help.

Blueberries are well suited for many culinary situations, but love is well suited for all life situations. As God showers us with His love, we can in turn express that love whenever and wherever we can, in many ways and in many situations. Amen!

Prayer Thought:

Dear God, let me show my love always and in all ways.

12

BUTTERFLY

Subject: Preparing for Easter

Object Item: A silk butterfly

Bible Verse: And we, who with unveiled faces all reflect the Lord's glory, are being transformed into His likeness with ever increasing glory, which comes from the Lord, who is the Spirit. (2 Corinthians 3:18)

Discussion:

Have you ever considered how a butterfly comes into existence? They burst forth from the cocoon within which they were sleeping. Some people use the butterfly as symbol for Easter. Jesus' resurrection from the tomb can be compared, in a small way, to the butterfly "resurrecting" from the cocoon. By looking at a butterfly, therefore, we are reminded of the reason that we celebrate Easter.

But if we look closer at the life of the butterfly, we can learn something even more important. You see, the butterfly starts out life as a caterpillar. After a while, the caterpillar makes a cocoon around itself, and something remarkable happens. A metamorphosis occurs. This is a big word that refers to the fact that the caterpillar actually changes its form and becomes a butterfly. The rather plain caterpillar is transformed into a magnificent butterfly.

When we ask Jesus to enter our hearts and become a part of our lives, He promises us that we too will change. "Old things are past. . . everything becomes new." Just like the butterfly, we become new creatures, better than we were because we are filled with God's spirit. The butterfly emerging from the cocoon reminds us of the <u>reason</u> for Easter, Jesus rising from the tomb. But as we approach Easter Sunday, we can see that the metamorphosis that happens in the cocoon reminds us of the <u>purpose</u> of Easter, the changing power of our risen Savior. Amen!

Prayer Thought:

Father, change me to your purpose.

13

EMPTY BASKET

Subject: The meaning of Easter

Object Item: An empty Easter basket

Bible Verse: Why do you look for the living among the dead? He is not here, He has risen! (Luke 24:5-6)

Discussion:

I imagine that Easter morning is pretty much the same in most homes. Children awake to find a basket filled with all manner of junk food and candy left for them by the Easter Bunny. Personally, no matter how old I get, I can't resist the urge to take one of those chocolate rabbits and bite the ears clean off. I used to get the same thrill with eating the entire head, but now I'm generally satisfied with just the ears. By the end of Easter Sunday, I'm sure that most of the candy is eaten and the plastic grass is strewn over the living room floor, leaving empty baskets in homes all over America.

As much as I enjoy the candy, eggs and other trappings of the holiday, I think that the empty basket symbolizes the meaning of Easter better than anything else. Remember that after He died on the cross, Jesus' body was laid in a tomb. Three days later, some women going to the tomb found that it was empty. As He had promised, Jesus had risen from the dead leaving the empty tomb. The empty basket reminds us of this empty tomb. The risen Lord gives us hope, that when we invite Jesus into our lives, He will be with us not only in this life, but forever. Amen!

Prayer Thought:

Father God, let the empty tomb remind me of life conquering death and of the joyous life that we can live in Christ.

14

ANNUALS

Subject: Year long faith

Object Item: Annual flowers

Bible Verse: Therefore, go and make disciples of all nations, baptizing them in the name of the Father and the Son and the Holy Spirit, and teaching them to obey everything I have commanded you, and surely I will be with you always, to the very end of the age. (Matthew 28:19-20)

Discussion:

There are all types of flowers, and all of them have their own kind of beauty. There are certain types of flowers, called annuals, that I find very interesting. These flowers are special because they only bloom once a year, and then, only for a very short time. Although these flowers are among the prettiest of all, sadly, they only show their beauty for a little while.

The time of the year following Easter is also very interesting. We are all uplifted by the excitement that surrounds this most sacred of our Christian holidays. Remembering Christ's resurrection from the tomb fills us with a renewed faith and commitment to Jesus. Yet, sometimes as the weeks pass after Easter, we get caught up with all the other things in our life, and little by little, we can begin to forget the beauty the we felt at Easter. Like the annual flower, our faith appears for a short while, then it begins to fade.

Faith in God is something that must be practiced all the time, for the entire year. We must carry the wonder of Easter with us always. Annual flowers bloom brightly then die, but our faith can bloom constantly and never die. Amen!

Prayer Thought:

Lord, prepare in my heart a lasting faith.

15

CLAY

Subject: The benefit of trials

Object Item: A hardened clay pot

Bible Verse: So do not fear, for I am with you; do not be dismayed for I am your God.   I will strengthen you and help you; I will uphold you with my righteous right hand. (Isaiah 41:10)

Discussion:

Have you ever seen how a piece of pottery is made? The pot is made of clay. As it is being formed, the clay is very soft and malleable. The pot of clay may look something like the final product, but it is still soft, and cannot serve the useful purpose of the final piece. In order for the pot to get hard it is placed in a very hot furnace called a kiln, and it is "fired" under a high temperature baking process. When it is removed from the kiln, it is then covered with a colored glaze and placed again into the kiln where it is fired again. Only after the clay is put through the fire twice can the piece be put to use.

Many times things in our lives don't go as we would like. Sometimes things happen that cause us emotional or physical pain. No one likes for bad things to happen to them. But we know that God will be right with us through these times in our lives. He will give us hope that no matter what happens to us, He will take care of us. And as the bad times go away, we are made stronger, and we are even more useful to God for his service. No one wants to go through bad times, but with God, these times in our lives can help us to be stronger in our faith. Amen!

Prayer Thought:

Lord, cover my weakness with your strength.

16

DISKETTE

Subject: God is there when we need Him

Object Item: A computer diskette

Bible Verse: For everything that was written in the past was written to teach us so that through endurance and the encouragement of the scriptures we might have hope. (Romans 15:4)

Discussion:

Take a close look at a computer diskette. It is only 3.5 inches on each side. Yet a normal disk can store more than 1.4 million pieces of information called "bytes." When you want to use the information stored on the disk, you just put it into a slot in the computer, the disk drive, and ask the computer to read the information from the disk and "load" it into the computer. We can then work with the information that was on the disk.

There are thousands of computer programs stored on disks, and they can do everything from drawing pictures to writing stories to performing complicated calculations. When you are finished with the information, you can store any changes that you made back onto the disk for use the next time that you want it.

God's word, the Bible, is somewhat like the computer disk described above. The word of God is "stored" in the pages of the New and Old Testaments. The books of the Bible contain the greatest story ever told; the story of God and how He has loved and related to His people. Not only do we learn about the great people of faith, but we learn about God and His purpose for us. We can learn how to live day to day. Further, these lessons are there anytime that we need them. We can "load" the information to our minds by reading God's word often and asking God to help us understand the wonderful lessons to be learned. Amen!

Prayer Thought:

Lord, give us hearts that hunger for your word.

17

GOOD TIMES AND BAD TIMES

Subject: God is with us all the time

Object Item: The sports section of the Sunday newspaper

Bible Verse: God is our refuge and strength, an ever present help in trouble. Therefore, we will not fear. (Psalms 45: 1-2)

Discussion:

I look forward to picking up the Sunday newspaper. It is filled with many sections that I enjoy reading including the comics, the travel section, the local news, etc. But my favorite section by far is the sports section. I am an avid sports fan and I like to follow the exploits of my favorite teams. Usually, when my team wins, I am very happy and I look forward to reading every story about the victory. But when they lose, I am much less eager to read very much, and I usually settle for a quick read of the statistics. That's the way it is with a sports team; sometimes you feel good and sometimes you feel bad.

Our lives are a lot like this. We have our ups and downs. When good things happen to us we feel happy and joyful, we smile and laugh. But when bad things happen, and they eventually happen to everyone, we feel sad and lonely. We think that no one has ever hurt as much as we do. And even though we know that it is very normal to feel this way, we still find it difficult to deal with the hurt. The good news is that God fully understands our feelings. He is with us when we feel good, sharing the experience of joy, and by doing this, increasing the joy that we feel. But more importantly, when bad things happen and we are sad, He is right there with us, and in His presence we can take comfort knowing that He shares our pain. He gives us hope that even as we feel bad, we also know that He loves us and will never stop loving us. Amen!

Prayer Thought:

Dear God, help us to look to you in both good times and bad.

18

INSIDE

Subject: The importance of what is inside our hearts

Object Item: A disk controller card, a microchip or other inside part of a computer

Bible Verse: Blind Pharisees! First clean the inside of the cup and dish, and then the outside will also be clean.   (Matthew 23:26)

Discussion:

The things on the inside of a computer look pretty weird. There are a lot of wires, silicone chips, plugs and other "high-tech" stuff.   When we look at a computer we see the monitor screen, the keyboard, the mouse and other neat looking things. But the real work of a computer is done by the "stuff" on the inside.   The things on the outside may look nicer, but the important elements are out of sight, inside the box.

People are a lot like this.   Although it is nice to look good on the outside, the things that we carry inside, in our hearts, are much more important. Our hearts should be filled with God's love. Jesus talked about certain people that are "clean" on the outside. They dress the right way, and say the right things, when all the time their hearts are evil. They care only about themselves, and their hearts are filled only with darkness.

We should, therefore, not judge one another by our outside appearance. Instead, we should seek to know each other on the inside, to know our hearts. For ourselves, we should love God, filling our hearts with His love, and sharing this love with others. Amen!

Prayer Thought:

Dear God, give me a clean heart to make me clean on the inside.

19

LOOK ALIKE

Subject: To be Christlike

Object Item: A picture of someone who looks like someone else

Bible Verse: Never be lacking in zeal, but keep your spiritual fervor, serving the Lord. (Romans 12:4)

Discussion:

Have you ever heard someone say that a child looks just like their parent? Certainly the child is not a perfect copy of the parent in every way. But the child may bear a strong resemblance, or he/she may have some attributes (intelligence, kindness, ambition etc.) held by parents. People will often compare people to animals or inanimate objects. For example, a person may be fast as a rabbit, strong as an ox, or steady as a rock. Of course we don't mean to say that people are just like the animals or the rock, but we make the comparisons to describe positive attributes common to rabbits, oxen and a rock.

The Bible tells us that we are to be like Christ. In fact the word "Christian" is Greek for "Christ Like." But Jesus is God; He healed the sick, made the blind to see, made the lame walk. He actually rose from the dead. Certainly we can not expect to be like Christ in these ways. But we can take to heart the positive attributes that Jesus exhibited while on earth. We can show kindness to all, give of ourselves to help others and most of all to serve rather than to be served. Even though Jesus was God, as a man on earth He came to serve those around Him who needed Him. The best way that we can serve Him is to be like Him and to serve others. Amen!

Prayer Thought:

Dear Jesus, help us to be more like you.

20

NUMBERS

Subject: God knows and loves us all

Object Item: Various meaningful numbers (e.g. social security, student I.D., etc.)

Bible Verse: God so loved the world that He gave us His only Son. (John 3:16)

Discussion:

All of us are known by many numbers. My student number in college was "61092." Whenever grades were posted on the department bulletin board, they were listed not by the students' names, but by their student numbers. At my place of work I am known as employee number "66341." Every week I turn in my time card, and even though my name is on the card, the accounting department will send it back to me if I fail to include my employee number. The company computers don't know my name, they know me as a number. Even the United States government refers to me by my social security number, and not by my name.

All the world's organizations use numbers to keep track of their members. Though this is very efficient, it is at best, impersonal, and at worst, dehumanizing. Isn't it wonderful that our God doesn't work this way. There are billions of people in the world. The Bible tells us that God knows every one of these people by name. Further, He knows all about us; what we like and dislike; what makes us happy and where we hurt; the good things and the not so good. The really wonderful thing is that because of what He knows, or in spite of it, He loves us more than anyone else can. Bill and Gloria Gaither wrote a song called We Are Loved that includes a line that says;

I am loved, I am loved, I can risk loving you.
For the One who knows me best loves me the most.

God knows us. He loves us. We can then, love in His name. Amen!

Prayer Thought:

Dear God, let me feel your love, then let me share your love.

21

THE RACE

Subject: Exercising your faith

Object Item: Something relating to a footrace

Bible Verse: Everyone who competes in the games goes into strict training. They do it to get a crown that will not last; but we do it to get a crown that will last forever. (1 Corinthians 9:25)

Discussion:

Have you ever watched a footrace? Although some races, like the Marathon, last for several hours, other races, like the 100 meter dash, are over in less than 10 seconds. Regardless of the length of the race, the people who participate in these races train and prepare for a long time, sometimes for years, so that they can perform at their best during the race. If an athlete stops practicing, even for a little while, he or she will not perform as well when the race comes.

St. Paul in his letter to the Corinthian church compared the Christian life to a race. We must prepare for this life as we would prepare for a race. But instead of strengthening our physical bodies, we must work to build up our spiritual bodies. We do this by learning God's word as it is presented in the Bible, by talking regularly to God in prayer and by exercising our faith by acting upon it to help those who are in need of God's care.

An athlete must train and prepare in order to win the race. So, too, must we prepare to compete in the race that life brings us. Amen!

Prayer Thought:

Lord, strengthen my faith.

22

SHOE BOX

Subject: Judging others

Object Item: A shoe box containing something other than shoes.

Bible Verse: Therefore, let us stop passing judgement on one another.   Instead, make up your mind not to put any stumbling block or obstacle in your brother's way. (Romans 14:13)

Discussion:

Look at a shoe box. It is just the right size for holding a pair of shoes. The words printed on the outside clearly indicate the contents of the box. A shoe box contains shoes. . . and that is that. (Open the box, however, and show that the box contains something other than shoes.) Without looking inside, you can't really know for sure what is contained in the shoe box. Your preconceived judgment can be proven wrong once you take a closer look.

You can't always judge something or someone just by the way that they look. Further, you <u>shouldn't</u> judge people or situations simply by the way that they appear to you. Although people aren't perfect and may be wrong about certain things, your perception of what they do may also be wrong. Rather than immediately judging people, we should love and accept them. Even if we don't always agree with what they say or do, we should still love them as people. God is the final judge of people, and He wants us to love Him by loving and not judging others. Amen!

Prayer Thought:

Father, you are the judge of the world. Help me to love, not to judge.

23

MOM

Subject: God's gift to us...our mothers (Mothers Day)

Object Item: A real mom, sitting on a stool

Bible Verse: . . . honor your father and mother, and love your neighbor as yourself. (Matthew 19:19)

Discussion:

Behold a typical All American mom! They are the most remarkable of God's creations. Moms are just different than any other type of human being. Consider that moms have;

- Eyes that see only the best in their children . . . even when seeing the good is not all that easy

- Ears that can hear a baby cry and know immediately their need . . . and then go to meet that need

- Lips that speak and sing softly to a sleeping child

- Arms always ready to embrace the child who won their first game, or lost their first love

- Hands that can be soft or firm . . . that mold a child's character from their first breath

- A heart that never empties

I believe that God gave us mothers so that we can see how much He cares about us. Moms are a window through which we can peek and get a glimpse of the Almighty. I love my mom . . . my children love their mom . . . God knows, they love us. Amen!

Prayer Thought:

Lord, help me to see your love in my mother and father.

24

STUFFING

Subject: Being filled with the Holy Spirit

Object Item: A stuffed animal and a bag of loose stuffing

Bible Verse: They saw what seemed to be tongues of fire that separated and came to rest on each of them. All of them were filled with the Holy Spirit. (Acts 2:3-4)

Discussion:

I suppose that all children love stuffed animals. They are cuddly and soft, and make very good friends. But consider what a stuffed animal would be like without the stuffing inside. It would be small and limp and have none of the endearing qualities that we have come to expect and enjoy. It might look a bit attractive, but it would not be filled out and complete. It is only complete when it is filled with the stuffing.

After Jesus died, His followers became very afraid. Even though they believed in Jesus and knew that He was God, they felt alone after he left them, and they were frightened that they

47

would not be able to follow His teachings now that He was no longer among them. You might say that like the unstuffed animal, they too were not complete.

God recognized their problem, and he solved it by sending His Holy Spirit to fill them. After they were filled with the spirit, they became complete followers and became effective witnesses for Christ. For us to be complete in the faith, we must also be filled with God's love and His Spirit. When we are, we are able to work for Him, and do His work on earth. Amen!

Prayer Thought:

Father, make me an empty vessel to be filled with your Holy Spirit.

25

TOOLS

Subject: We can be tools of God for his purpose.

Object Item: A box of tools

Bible Verse: It was He who gave some to be apostles, some to be prophets, some to be evangelists and some to be pastors and teachers. (Ephesians 4:11)

Discussion:

A well stocked tool box contains a tool for most every job. My tool box, when everything is where it is supposed to be, holds all types of screwdrivers, a wide assortment of wrenches, a hammer, a saw and more "do-dads" than I can mention. When I have a job to do, I look into the box and search for just the right tool that will be able to best help me complete the work. If I wanted to turn a screw, it would do me no good to grab a hammer. But with the right tool, I can easily do the job.

God wants to do many good things in our world. More often than not, He uses us, His children, to get the job done. We can be tools for good in God's hand. Like the different tools in the box, we all have different abilities and gifts that God can use for different tasks. If you are a doctor, He may ask you to help Him heal. If you are a good cook, He may ask you to help feed the hungry. If you are blessed with a great deal of money, He may ask you to share it with the poor.

We are responsible for making sure that we are available for God to use when He needs us. That means we should talk to Him (pray) often, and listen for His response to us. If we develop the talents He has given us and are sensitive to His leading, we can be useful tools for God's work. Amen!

Prayer Thought:

Lord, help me to know my gifts and to use them to your purpose

26

UNIFORMS

Subject: How we are identified as Christians

Object Item: A Uniform

Bible Verse: Therefore, put on the full armor of God.
(Ephesians 6:13)

Discussion:

While watching a sporting event, how can you distinguish one team from another? The answer is really simple. All the players on a particular team wear the same uniforms. Many teams are not only identified by their uniforms, but what they wear helps define their character. The Big Red Machine, Celtic Green, Dodger Blue, The Crimson Tide and countless other terms mean much more to these teams than just the color of the uniforms.

What would you say is the uniform of a Christian? Can you easily identify a follower of Christ by looking at their clothes? Maybe a Christian uniform is a choir robe, or a Sunday dress, or maybe a three piece suit. Actually, the Apostle Paul tells us something about a Christian uniform in his letter to the Ephesians. But he doesn't talk about clothes. He tells us that our uniform is not what we wear, but rather what we are and do. Faith, righteousness, love, salvation and studying God's word are the things that identify us as Christians. We should understand how to acquire this "uniform" and how to wear it as we represent Jesus in our everyday lives. Amen!

Prayer Thought:

Lord, help me to be strong in my faith and to wear your armor.

27

FLAG

Subject: The importance (and limitations) of symbols

Object Item: An American flag

Bible Verse: Let us fix our eyes on Jesus, the author and perfection of our faith, who for the joy set before Him, endured the cross. (Hebrews 12:12)

Discussion:

I like patriotic holidays. One of my favorite parts of these celebrations involves flying the American flag. On Memorial Day or Independence Day, many of the houses in my neighborhood display the flag outside their homes. The flag stands as a symbol of freedom, equality, democracy and liberty; all the positive and good things about our country. As we look at the flags flying, we should remember that without all of these things that the flag represents, it would be nothing more than a pretty piece of cloth.

As Christians we have symbols that relate to our faith. Look at the cross. It reminds us of the ultimate sacrifice that Jesus made for us. It helps us to remember that Jesus loves us all, and promises us a wonderful life if we ask Him into our hearts. Without these things, the cross is just pieces of wood. The symbols that we hold dear to us are, in themselves, of little value without the important things that they symbolize. So every time we look at these symbols, the flag or the cross, let us take time to reflect and remember their deep meaning to us. Amen!

Prayer Thought:

Jesus, let me never forget what you did for me on the cross.

28

AUTOGRAPH

Subject: God has left His mark on our hearts

Object Item: An item with an autograph

Bible Verse: . . . so that Christ may dwell in your hearts through faith. (Ephesians 3:17)

Discussion:

Have you ever been to a professional sports event? There are always a lot of people that our trying to get the players to sign a program, a ball, a bat or other item that they carry to the game. The signature of the player is called an autograph. An autograph is valuable for a number of reasons. To a collector, a sports card of a player with his actual autograph is worth more money than an unsigned card. But to a fan, the real value is being able to claim that their sports hero touched the signed item. He sort of left a piece of himself with the fan. In a way, his presence is always with the fan.

As Christians, we ask Jesus to enter our hearts and to live in us. Jesus writes His name in our hearts. By doing this, He leaves a piece of Himself in our hearts and minds. His presence is always with us. His autograph on our lives is most valuable. With it, we are never alone, and we know that His love is with us and we can in turn love others in His name. Amen!

Prayer Thought:

Dear Jesus, fill my heart with your love.

29

CLOCK

Subject: Full time faith

Object Item: A clock

Bible Verse: Rejoice in the Lord always, I will say it again. Rejoice! (Phillipians 4:4)

Discussion:

We use clocks to measure time. There are all types of clocks; digital, analog, grandfather, even the kind that looks like a cat with his tail as the pendulum sweeping back and forth (my personal favorite). Clocks may look different but they all serve the same basic purpose: to tell time. Time is very important to all of us. For many people, there doesn't seem to be enough time to get everything that they need to get done. People who work either work full time or part time. Full time workers usually spend at least 8 hours per day, and usually more, at work. Most of these people will tell us that they are very busy with their work, and that they have little time for other activities.

Faith in God is not a part time activity. We should have a faith that is always alive and working, not only 8 hours, but 24 hours per day, every day. It is easy to have faith when things are going well. But when times are hard, we must take care to keep our faith. In fact, these are the times when our faith is most important. The Bible tells us to rejoice always, in good times and bad. Let us learn to have a full time faith in God. Amen!

Prayer Thought:

Dear Lord, let me look to you at all times

30

DISPOSABLE

Subject: Our faith in God is forever

Object Item: A disposable, single use pen and a refillable pen

Bible Verse: . . . and once made perfect, He became the source of eternal salvation for all who obey Him. (Hebrews 5:9)

Discussion:

As a child in grade school, I remember using a refillable fountain pen for all my school work. When it ran out of ink, we had to remove an empty cartridge from the pen and replace it with a new cartridge that was full of ink. Around the fourth grade, I was introduced to the phenomenon of the disposable pen. This new pen, produced by the Bic Company, took the writing world by storm. No longer did we have to worry about refilling our pens. Instead, we simply used them until they ran out of ink, and then we tossed them into the garbage can and took out a new one.

Nowadays, it seems that most everything that we use has a disposable counterpart. I often will use a disposal razor while on a business trip, and we frequently use disposable forks and knives during summer bar-b-ques. Disposable diapers are much more popular than cloth diapers, and I've even owned a disposable electronic calculator. None of these items are built to last very long. Instead, they get quickly used up and thrown away.

Although it may be all right for some of the trivial articles in our lives to be used up and discarded, the important things are meant to last. The love we have for each other should be nurtured and tended so that it grows every day. Our faith in God, also, is not disposable. It cannot be used up and discarded when we think we are finished. Rather, as we exercise our faith, it will grow stronger and stronger, and it will always be with us; forever. Amen!

Prayer Thought:

Heavenly Father, help me to keep my faith in you, now and forever

31

HATS

Subject: The role of the father (Father's Day)

Object Item: Various types of hats

Bible Verse: . . . for your Father knows what you need before you ask Him. (Matthew: 6:8)

Discussion:

I have a lot of hats in my house. In fact, I am somewhat of a hat collector. I have over one hundred baseball caps, most of which advertise some company or organization. But the hats that I like the best are the ones that serve practical purposes. I have a hard hat that I sometimes use at work, and it protects me from head injuries on the job. My golf hat is made of straw and it has a wide brim to keep the sun off my head and neck. My Atlanta Braves cap lets people know that I am a fan of that team. I wear different hats at different times.

As a father, I also have to "wear different hats" for my children. They have different needs that depend on various situations. When they need to learn about life, I am a teacher. When they behave inappropriately, I am a disciplinarian. When they are troubled, I am their friend. A good father must be many different people to his children.

Our Father in heaven is even more present for us all in whatever form that we need Him. No matter what our need, He meets it as a perfect Father. He perfectly wears any hat that we need. Amen!

Prayer Thought:

Father God, help me know that I can rely on you for anything that I need.

32

INSTRUCTIONS

Subject: Seeking God's help

Object Item: Assembly instructions

Bible Verse: Let us then approach the throne of grace with confidence so that we may receive mercy and find grace to help us in time of need. (Hebrews 4:16)

Discussion:

The three words most feared by parents are "Some Assembly Required." Many a dad has found himself on Christmas Eve, mumbling amidst a pile of bolts, screws, pins, wires and sundry bicycle parts, regretting his decision to save the ten dollars that the store would have charged to assemble his purchase. Most of the problems with assembly arise from a stubborn tendency to ignore the assembly instructions. I am especially adept at setting the instructions down and taking on the bicycle using a pair of pliers, an adjustable wrench and my own devices.

Most of the time I'm left with only a few leftover pieces. After all, don't they always put extra stuff in the box in case some pieces are lost? Actually, when we try to assemble the item without the help offered by the instructions, we are, more often than not, doomed to failure.

In our everyday lives we are faced with decisions that affect the way that we do things and how we relate to the people in our lives. We may choose to study a situation closely before we make a decision, or we may decide quickly, based solely on our instincts (the so called "going with the gut"). However we decide, we often overlook a critical source of help. God is there whenever we need Him, and He is ready and willing to offer us advice regarding a decision, no matter how small or important. All we need to do is to ask for His guidance and He will find a way to help us out. How much better it is to embark into the unknown when we have God's advice in our pocket. Amen!

Prayer Thought:

Dear Lord, may we look to you and your word in our times of decision.

33

PATTERN

Subject: We are all pieces of God's plan

Object Item: A Dress Pattern

Bible Verse: . . . so in Christ we who are many form one body, and each member belongs to all the others. (Romans 12:5)

Discussion:

When I was a child, my bedroom also served as my mother's sewing room. Many days I was awakened by my mother tinkering at her machine. I remember vividly the dozens of dress pattern pieces that were frequently strewn over my bed. These tissue paper like pieces seemed to find their way into my pillows, dresser drawers, and places in my room that I didn't even know existed. Strangely, none of these odd shaped pieces by themselves looked anything like a dress. But my mom's exceptional skill soon made these disjointed pieces into a beautiful dress.

All of us are like these individual pattern pieces. We are in many ways, frail and disjointed. We are all different. Yet, we are all part of God's great pattern of life. By ourselves we do not complete God's purpose, but when we put ourselves into His hands, He can turn the many, different, frail and separate pieces into His grand plan. Amen!

Prayer Thought:

Lord, make me a part of your plan.

34

SALT

Subject: Christians in the world

Object Item: A salt shaker filled with salt

Bible Verse: You are the salt of the earth. But if the salt loses its saltiness, can it be made salty again? (Matthew 5:13)

Discussion:

Salt is the most common seasoning that we use. Salt is so popular that some people even collect salt shakers that are in all kinds of shapes. We use salt to add flavoring to otherwise bland food. I can't imagine eating french fries without salt. In ancient times, salt was used for other purposes. In those days the people didn't have refrigerators to keep food from spoiling. Instead, they used salt to preserve meat. Although it probably tasted a bit salty, it didn't spoil.

Jesus once said that His followers were to be the "salt of the earth." By this He meant that as his followers, we help preserve the world from spoiling and going bad. Also, living the life that

Christ wants from us helps "flavor" the world by making it more meaningful and exciting. As Christians we should be like salt and season the world with God's love. Amen!

Prayer Thought:

Lord Jesus, help me to spread your word and season the world with your love.

35

SIGNS

Subject: We are like signs for God

Object Item: A sign

Bible Verse: Then the disciples went out and preached everywhere, and the Lord worked with them and confirmed His word by the signs that accompanied it. (Mark 16:20)

Discussion:

Have you ever walked by a store window filled with signs advertising the items that are inside, or announcing a big sale? You know right away, by looking at the signs, that something is going on inside. When you see a sign that says "Closed," you know that you will not be able to shop at that store. Signs in the window tell you when the store will be open, or what type of goods that are sold inside. Signs are very helpful in that they give us valuable information.

When Jesus was on earth, He performed miracles. Some referred to these miracles as "signs" that He was the Messiah.

Just like a "Sale" sign tells that a sale is going on, Jesus' miracles told that He was God. His actions were a sign of His divinity. The way we act can also be a sign of who we are. If we act badly, we are like a sign that says "Beware, stay away." But if we conduct ourselves in a way that pleases God, according to His law, then our lives will be like a sign that says, "Jesus Lives Here." Amen!

Prayer Thought:

Dear God, help me to live my life so that people will know that Jesus is in my heart.

36

PAPER TOWEL

Subject: Jesus' place in our lives

Object Item: A roll of paper towels.

Bible Verse: And in Him you too are being built together to become a dwelling in which God lives by His Spirit. (Ephesians 2:22)

Discussion:

Take a close look at a roll of paper towels. Specifically look at the cardboard tube in the center. Along with serving as a great "toot toot" horn when the roll is finished, the tube also has a useful purpose. This tube keeps the roll of towels in a usable shape. If the tube were to be removed the roll would collapse and the towels would not dispense easily off the roll.

Jesus is something like the tube. When He is at the center of our lives our lives can be complete and in order. But if He is not there, our lives may "collapse" and unravel. Just as the tube is most important at the center of the towels, so too is Jesus most important at the center of our lives. Amen!

Prayer Thought:

Lord Jesus, always be in the center of my life and my being.

37

WALKMAN

Subject: God listens to us always

Object Item: A portable stereo and headphones

Bible Verse: The Lord is near to all who call on Him, to all who call on Him in truth. (Psalms 145:18)

Discussion:

I am constantly amazed with the ability of stereo makers to continually reduce the size of their products. When I was younger, I would listen to my music on a stereo system that fit on three separate shelves in my room. The speakers alone were about 2 feet high. This system wasn't exactly portable, and if I wanted to listen to my music, I was pretty much restricted to staying in my room. Today, people put on their headphones, slip a CD into the player hooked onto their belts, and go on their merry way. Folks can listen to their music anywhere and anytime they want.

I also used to think that we could talk to God only at certain times or in specific places, such as in church on Sunday, before meals, or during certain mid-term exams. But as I grew older I came to realize that this isn't true. We can talk to God at home, at school, on the golf course or anywhere else. Also, we don't have to wait for a predetermined time. You see, God is <u>always</u> listening for us. When we seek to talk to Him, we never get a busy signal. God cares about us and He is always ready to listen for and talk to us. Amen!

Prayer Thought:

Heavenly Father, thank you for always listening, anywhere and anytime.

38

BALOON

Subject: God's presence in us

Object Item: An unfilled balloon

Bible Verse: Make every effort to live in peace with all men and to be holy; without holiness no one will see the Lord. (Hebrews 12:14)

Discussion:

An unfilled balloon is not very interesting. When you blow up a balloon it expands with the air inside. By releasing the air, the balloon again becomes flat. Where did the air go? You cannot see the air either filling or exiting the balloon. By itself the air is invisible. But the expanded balloon clearly looks different than the uninflated balloon. The presence of the air, although unseen, makes an obvious difference.

We cannot generally see God in a physical way. Some artists have painted Him, mostly as a kindly old man. Sort of a Santa Clause in white robes. But really, He doesn't often make

Himself visible to us. However, people can see the presence of God; they can see God in us. By loving each other and living according to God's will, people can see an invisible God become visible through our lives. Amen!

Prayer Thought:

Dear Jesus, help me to feel you in my heart so others can see you in me.

39

CATS

Subject: God's forgiveness

Object Item: A stuffed cat toy or a picture of a cat

Bible Verse: But we had to celebrate and be glad because this brother of yours was dead and is alive again; he was lost and is found. (Luke 15:32)

Discussion:

I have always had cats around my house. Cats are very interesting animals. They pretty much take care of themselves, and most of them have a very independent streak. Once I had a cat that would occasionally leave for a few days. I would worry where he went, and whether he would ever return. After a few days he would find his way to my back door, and instead of being angry that he had run away, I was relieved that he was safe again in my house. Even after the cat had done this several times, I always welcomed him back.

Jesus tells a story about a man who had two sons. One of the boys asked his father for his share of his inheritance and left home. He quickly squandered all his money, spending it all on wild living. He soon became penniless and was forced to live and eat with pigs. He then realized the error of his ways and knew that what he had done was wrong. Even the servants in his father's house were better off than he was. So he returned home to be with his father. When his father saw him coming, he wasn't angry. Instead, he rejoiced that the son, who he thought was lost, had returned.

God is like the father. We are like the son (or the cat) and we often turn away from God and do things that hurt Him. Sometimes we are more concerned with ourselves than with God's will. But if we turn away from our wrongdoing and turn back to God, He will always welcome us back, and His love for us will not be diminished. God's capacity to forgive us is beyond anything that we can measure, if we just ask for it. Amen!

Prayer Thought:

Father God, I pray that I do not sin, but, know that you will still love and forgive me if I do.

40

<u>*BACK TO SCHOOL*</u>

Subject: Spiritual and life tools

Object Item: A bag of school supplies

Bible Verse: All scripture is God breathed and is useful for teaching, rebuking, correcting and training in righteousness, so that the man of God may be thoroughly equipped for every good work. (2 Tim. 3:16-17)

Discussion:

Have you ever visited an office supply store with your parents just before you begin a new school year? You walk in with lists in hand, walking up and down the aisles and filling the cart with pens, pencils, notebooks, binders, glue sticks, assignment pads, calculators and all manner of supplies needed to face the new year. Students are provided with all these tools so that they can both learn and express themselves as part of their learning experiences. Children will perform better if they have the proper tools, and parents are responsible for getting these tools for them.

We approach our lives in much the same way as children approach a new school year. They need the proper tools in order to perform well. In order to live a life pleasing to God, we must be equipped with the proper tools and supplies. Through studying God's word, we learn of God's love for us, and that because we are loved, we can learn how to use the most important tools of life; love, compassion, understanding, tolerance, caring and all the good things that God uses to equip His children. Amen!

Prayer Thought:

Father, equip us with your love to do good works in your name

41

ICEBERG

Subject: God's hidden servants

Object Item: A picture of an iceberg

Bible Verse: . . . then your Father who sees what is done in secret, will reward you. (Matthew 6:6)

Discussion:

Have you ever seen a picture of an iceberg? They are huge pieces of ice that have broken off a glacier and float in the cold Arctic waters. They are very pretty and majestic as they tower over the ocean below. But they pose a constant threat to ships passing by them because no matter how big the iceberg appears above the surface, only about ten percent of an iceberg can be seen. The biggest part lies below the water, completely unseen by passing ships. Even though it can't be seen, the biggest part of the iceberg is still there, right below the surface.

Take a look at the people in our church who serve God: preachers, lay leaders, missionaries, singers etc. We constantly see these individuals, and we are grateful for their commitment and service. But there are many more of God's servants whom we cannot see. These are regular people who live their lives according to Christ every day. They love their fellow man, they care about one another, and make sacrifices for others above themselves. No one ever notices them, nor are they often recognized for their contributions. But God, who sees in secret, knows of their faith, and rewards them in other ways. So for every servant that you see and recognize, there are many more who will never be noticed. But this is how God's work is done. Amen!

Prayer Thought:

Dear God, thank you for those who serve you in secret. Help them to know that their reward awaits them.

42

INVITATION

Subject: We are all invited to be part of God's family

Object Item: An invitation to a party

Bible Verse: He tends His flock like a shepherd: He gathers the lambs in His arms, and carries them close to His heart; (Isaiah 40:11)

Discussion

One of the nicest thing that can happen to a person is to receive an invitation to a party. You feel special that someone wants you to share in a happy occasion in their lives. An invitation usually includes a note to RSVP. This means that if you are going to go to the party you need to call the person who invited you to tell them that you are going to attend. In other words, you have to respond. If you choose to attend, most of the time you are expected to bring a present for the guest of honor.

As nice as it is to be invited, it can be very disappointing to be left out of a party. You feel very bad if you are not invited while some of your friends have been. You don't feel very special then.

In a way, God is always having a party. He invites all of us to be a part of it. In this way, He shows us that we are all very special. We are all invited to follow Him and to be a member of His family. All we have to do is to respond. We just have to say "yes" to God's invitation. We don't even have to bring a present. God only wants <u>us</u>, and He loves us just as we are. Amen!

Prayer Thought:

Lord, help me to be worthy of your invitation.

43

RESTS

Subject: Taking time to rest

Object Item: A music score showing a rest

Bible Verse: Come to me all who are weary and heavy laden and I will give you rest. (Matthew 11:28)

Discussion:

If you look at a musical score you can see that the music is made up of many different types of notes. The score also includes treble and bass clefs, repeat signs, dynamic marks, and lots of Italian words that tell the musician how to play or sing the music. One of the most underrated parts of the musical score is the rest. A rest is put in the music to tell the musician when <u>not</u> to play. Sometimes the rest allows another part to be heard better, and sometimes it just lets everyone rest for a moment, just to listen.

During the business of our busy days, we constantly work to play the "music" of life. We repeatedly try to please ourselves or others, endeavoring to constantly improve ourselves. Working hard is good, and we should always try our best at everything that we do. But life is also meant to have rests. We have to take time to stop ourselves and just listen; listen to our children, our friends, the wind . . . and the voice of God. God wants to talk to us, to tell us how He feels about things, and how much He loves and cares for us. But unless we stop, <u>rest</u>, and listen, we may not be able to hear Him. Rest awhile . . . and listen for God! Amen!

Prayer Thought:

Father God, teach me to rest and, while I rest, help me to hear you.

44

TELEPHONE BOOK

Subject: God knows and cares about all of us

Object Item: A large telephone book

Bible Verse: I am the good shepherd; I know my sheep and my sheep know me. . . (John 10:14)

Discussion:

Did you ever take a close look at a major metropolitan phone book? There are tens, even hundreds of thousands of names in the book. I have looked at books that had over twenty pages of a single last name. Whenever I go to a new city, I check the phone book to see if there are any people listed who have the same last name as I. It's not that I would ever call these people, I just feel better knowing that there are people who are, in some way, like me. When I look in my home city phone book, I recognize only a few names of people I know. Even those of us with a lot of friends can claim to know only a very small fraction of the people listed in the book.

Jesus tells us that our Father in heaven can number us as the sands of the desert, the hairs on our head or the stars in the sky. In fact, God knows every single person listed in every phone book in the world. Furthermore, He loves and cares about every one. God's knowledge and love have no bounds. Every one of us is very special and unique in God's eyes. When we feel that we are alone and that no one cares about us, we can remember the millions of people in the phone books, and how God knows and cares about us among all these people. We are special! Amen!

Prayer Thought:

Dear Lord, I know that you know the real me, and you love me in spite of my flaws. Thank you.

45

SOCCER AND GOLF

Subject: The body of the church

Object Item: A soccer ball and a golf ball

Bible Verse: There are different kinds of gifts, but the same Spirit. There are different kinds of service but the same Lord. (1 Cor. 12: 4-5)

Discussion:

During a recent weekend I was "surfing" through the channels of my television set and began watching a World Cup soccer game. I admit that I do not know very much about the game, but I was taken by the amazing teamwork exhibited by the players on both teams. Every player at his respective position had a different role to play. The goalkeeper's job was to prevent the opposing team from putting the ball in his goal. The defenders hindered the advancing team by trying to steal the ball. The midfielders passed the ball from the defensive to the offensive zone, while the forwards carried the ball towards the opponent's goal and tried to score the goals. It was clear that success could be achieved only if every member of the team worked together.

During halftime I switched over to watch a golf tournament and I was struck by the contrast between the two competitions that I was watching. Golf is a solitary game. Success depends upon the skills of the individual. There are no teammates upon whom to depend. When one of the golfers made a mistake he had to live with it and correct it himself.

The church of Jesus Christ is much more like a soccer team than a golfer. Every Christian has special gifts and abilities and plays their own separate roles in the church. We are teachers, preachers, helpers, healers or one of many other servers of our Lord. All of our contributions are important. Alone our gifts are not adequate, but together our abilities combine in a whole that, with God's help, is greater than the sum of the parts. Together, seeking God's will, we form the Church, and we have the opportunity and the ability to win the world for Christ. Amen!

Prayer Thought:

God, show me my gifts and talents, then teach me how to use them in your service.

46

DIFFERENCES

Subject: The unity of spirit in the church

Object Item: Two teddy bears that don't look alike

Bible Verse: Here there is no Greek or Jew, circumcised or uncircumcised, barbarian, Scythian, slave or free, but Christ is all, and is in all. (Colossians 3:11)

Discussion:

My children have always had a fascination with teddy bears. One look in their rooms tells the visitor that these cute stuffed bears are very important to my kids. Even though they have so many bears, they all look a bit different; different sizes and colors, wearing different clothes. They are all unique. If you look at a group of children, it is also clear that they are all unique, and that they look different. Some are boys, some are girls, some are tall others are short, some have brown eyes while some have blue eyes and they might have brown, black, yellow, red or white skin

On any given day there are people all over the world worshiping our Lord. Now, I haven't been to too many different churches, but I've been to enough to know that people worship in different ways. They sing different music, wear different clothes, preach in different ways and just generally do things differently. You may visit a different church and be very surprised with the way things are done. You might even be a bit uncomfortable. But the very good news about Christ's church is that even though we may worship in different ways, we are united by a singleness of purpose that is God's spirit. We who follow Christ worship the same God, and despite our differences, we are one in God's spirit. Amen!

Prayer Thought:

Dear Lord, make me appreciate the differences of all those who love with your Holy Spirit in their hearts.

47

FLYING A KITE

Subject: God's unfailing love

Object Item: A kite and a string

Bible Verse: Never will I leave you; never will I forsake you. (Hebrews 13:5)

Discussion:

I love flying a kite. Ever since I was a child, I have loved getting out on a windy day and holding on to the string while the kite tugged, dipped and flew high above me. Sometimes, when the kite is tossed to and fro it is hard to hold on to. Sometimes it rises high, and you have to let out string, or it dives, and you have to reel in the string very quickly. But as long as you hold on, the kite keeps flying. If you were to let go of the string, the kite would fly away or fall to the ground.

Much like kites, we are often tossed to and fro by the "winds" of life. Sometimes we are high and feeling good about things, and other times we are down and feel pretty bad.

Sometimes we soar and sometimes we dive. But no matter how we are, and how we are buffeted about, God never lets go of the "string" that holds us to Him. Sometimes He lets out the "string," and sometimes He has to "reel us in." But He loves us very much, and He will never let us go. As long as we trust in Him, He will always bring us back to where He wants us to be. Amen

Prayer Thought:

Father God, show me how to fly on the wind of your love and trust.

48

THANK YOU

Subject: Giving thanks to God

Object Item: Something depicting Thanksgiving

Bible Verse: Give thanks to the Lord for He is good; His love endures forever. (1 Chronicles 16:34)

Discussion:

While riding in the car one day, my kids and I wanted to see in how many languages we could say "thank you." We knew how to say "merci" (French), "gracias" (Spanish), "danke" (German), "grazi" (Italian) and "djenkuja" (Polish). There are many ways to say thank you without speaking at all. We thank people for presents by writing thank you notes. Sometimes we say thank you with a smile. I think that the best way to thank someone who has done something nice for us is to do something nice in turn for someone else.

On Thanksgiving we take time to thank God for all He has done for us. At our house our entire family gathers around a table loaded with turkey, ham, dressing, vegetables, pies and cakes, and we ask God to bless us and we thank Him for all the times He has blessed us in the past. I think that we <u>should</u> do this. Yet, I think that there are better ways to thank God. We can show our thanks by helping those in need by giving of ourselves to help the less fortunate, and by doing this in God's name. It is nice to <u>say</u> thank you to God, but it is even better to live our thanks. Amen!

Prayer Thought:

Lord, as I thank you with my lips and my heart, help me to thank you with my life.

49

<u>COMING ATTRACTIONS</u>

Subject: Advent: preparing for the Savior

Object Item: Movie section of the newspaper

Bible Verse: Prepare the way for the Lord, make straight paths for Him. (Matthew 3:3)

Discussion:

The movie section of the newspaper gives you good information regarding movies, when and where they are playing, and how much they cost. I must admit, I spend a good deal of time perusing the movie section because I really enjoy going to theaters to watch movies. I know that videos are more convenient, and that you can watch them in the comfort and privacy of your own home. But there is something about watching a film on the big screen that cannot be equaled on even the largest television set. I also confess that one of my favorite parts of the theater experience is the coming attractions that are shown before the main feature. These little pieces of movies let us know what upcoming movies are about, and when they are going to be shown in the theater. We can then plan our schedules and prepare to see the film.

We all know that December the 25th is Christmas, and on this day we celebrate God's ultimate gift to us; His son Jesus sent to earth as a little baby. The four Sundays before Christmas are known as Advent. Advent is sort of the "coming attractions" for Christmas. During this time we prepare ourselves to celebrate Christ's coming. During Advent, most churches have lots of opportunities to sing, give, study and worship in special ways. All these opportunities are wonderful, and we should take advantage of them.

I believe, though, that the best way that we can prepare for Jesus is to get to know Him better. We can study about the prophecies of His birth, learn about the purpose of His life and spend more time talking to Him. By getting to know Jesus better, we can become closer to Him and be prepared for Him at Christmas and throughout the year. Amen!

Prayer Thought:

Dear Jesus, help me to know you better so that I can prepare for your life within me.

50

WANTING

Subject: God provides our needs

Object Item: A Christmas List

Bible Verse: But seek first His kingdom and His righteousness, and all these things will be given to you as well. (Matthew 6:33)

Discussion:

Everybody in my family looks forward to Christmas. I think that my kids start talking about Christmas sometime around the Fourth of July. There is something about the prospect of a load of presents that gets them really interested in this particular holiday. Inevitably, a few weeks before Thanksgiving, the Christmas catalogs begin to arrive and everyone in the house begins to make up their list of preferred gifts. These "want" lists are left strategically around the house where they are sure to be noticed. Certainly children work hard to make sure that their wants are satisfied on Christmas morning, and more times than not, parents make sure that they are.

Some people think that God is somewhat like Santa Clause or like an indulging parent at Christmastime. They believe that all they need do is ask something of God, and He will provide for them. To them it really doesn't matter the nature of the request: God will provide for them. But God is not Santa Clause: He is <u>much</u> more than that. God loves us in a way that we can't understand. He has promised to provide us our every need. But we often don't need what we want. Sometimes our wants are not healthy for us and will eventually cause us harm or heartache. God knows what we need to fulfill our lives, and He will always make sure that these needs are met. Amen!

Prayer Thought:

Father God, teach me how to know my needs from my wants, and to want what you believe I need.

51

THE KINGS

Subject: God is accessible to us

Object Item: A picture or figurines of the "Three Kings"

Bible Verse: On coming to the house, they saw the child with His mother Mary, and they bowed down and worshiped Him. Then they opened their treasures and presented Him with gifts of gold and of incense and of myrrh. (Matthew 2:11)

Discussion:

One of the centerpieces of Christmas around my house is the manger scene that sits prominently in the living room. All the required figures are there. Little baby Jesus is in a manger, flanked by Mary and Joseph, with a donkey and a cow lying behind them. Several shepherds are standing or kneeling outside the stall, surrounded by a number of sleeping sheep. But my favorite figures are those of the Wise Men. Every manger scene that I have ever seen shows 3 well dressed Wise Men (or Kings) standing or kneeling, gifts in hand, with their camels close behind.

Now, the bible doesn't ever say that there were 3 Wise Men. All it says is that Wise Men came from the east to visit the baby Jesus. We do know that they must have come from a very long distance just to see this child. Remember that traveling in those days was a very difficult and trying experience. Riding on bumpy camels on dusty roads and through deserts, with no place to stay but in a tent, made traveling very hard. Yet, they made this sacrifice to see the God Child.

We are so fortunate! We don't have to travel hundreds of miles to see the Messiah. God has given us the gift of His son, Jesus, and all we have to do to know Him is to ask Him into our lives. God does not require us to bring gifts of gold or precious spices. He simply asks us to accept His gift to us. Amen!

Prayer Thought:

Jesus, even though I have no gift to lay before you, you have given me the gift of your life.

52

TRASH

Subject: The spirit of Christmas can last all year

Object Item: A garbage bag filled with used Christmas wrapping paper

Bible Verse: And surely I will be with you always, to the very end of the age. (Matthew 28:20)

Discussion:

Christmas morning is one of the most exciting times for children. To this day I remember running down the stairs from my bedroom and turning the corner into the living room to behold the indescribable mural of green, red and gold that was the mass of wrapped gifts under the tree. I would quickly find a package with my name on it, and I would tear off the wrapping with which my mother had so carefully and lovingly decorated my gift. A few minutes is all it took to obliterate hours of artistic creativity. The aftermath of my efforts lay strewn over the living room floor about 30 minutes after I had begun. All the beautiful wrapping and decorations that had adorned my booty was soon transformed into so much wastepaper trash.

Much of the celebration of Christmas is like the wrapping. The anticipation of the day soon gives way to the post-Christmas letdown and the drudgery of day to day living. This happens if we lose sight of the "reason for the season." But we don't have to do this. We can enjoy the trappings of the holiday all the more if we remember that God loves us so much that He sent His Son in the form of a little child. The parties eventually end, and the gifts eventually break, wear out, or are used up. But with Jesus in our hearts, we have the most important gift that we will ever receive; and the good news is that we have this gift with us, every day and forever. Amen

Prayer Thought:

Lord, live with me all the days of my life.

About the Author

By day, Mark L. Mongeau is a mild mannered, Professional Engineer, working for an engineering consulting firm in Orlando, Florida. Mark earned his Bachelors and Masters degrees in Civil Engineering from Rensselaer Polytechnic Institute, and has spent the last 25 years practicing as a geotechnical engineer in Florida and Ohio, (This means that he is an expert in dirt).

On the weekends, and especially on Sunday mornings, he is transformed into "Mr. Mark", and leads the children's sermons for the First United Methodist Church of Winter Park, Florida. Over the past 15 years he has delivered over 700 "Children's Moments" to a generation of children in Central Florida. In addition, he is a sought after lecturer and speaker on a wide range of topics including biblical exposition, public speaking, customer service, business development and geotechnical engineering. He lives in Oviedo, Florida with his wife Carol, and three children, Sarah, Rachel and Andrew.

Printed in the United States
2688